THE FROGS

By Aristophanes

a new adaptation by

David Muncaster

THE FROGS

INTRODUCTORY NOTE

Aristophanes is acknowledged as the greatest of the Greek comic writers and is the only one whose works has survived in complete form. He was born in Athens and had his first comedy produced when he was so young that his name was withheld on account of his youth. He is credited with over forty plays, eleven of which survive, along with the names and fragments of some twenty-six others. He died in 388 BC.

"The Frogs" was produced the year after the death of Euripides and laments the decay of Greek tragedy. It is an excellent example of his style, mingling wit and poetry with rowdy humour and a keen sense for satire. Through his hostility to Euripides and his attacks on Socrates, he makes it clear that he prefers tradition over innovation, whether that be in politics, religion, or art.

THE FROGS

CAST

A minimum of six actors play the following:

THE GOD DIONYSUS
XANTHIAS, his slave
AESCHYLUS
EURIPIDES
HERACLES
A CORPSE
CHARON
AEACUS, house porter to Pluto
A MAID
A LANDLADY IN HADES
PLATHANE, her servant
PLUTO
A CHORUS OF FROGS
A CHORUS OF THE INITIATED
CHORUS LEADER

THE FROGS

ACT ONE

SCENE ONE

Opening Music: XANTHIAS and DIONYSUS enter. DIONYSUS is dressed in a loincloth and carries a club. XANTHIAS is straining from carrying a load.

XANTHIAS: (*Spotting audience.*) Shall I crack a few of the old ones, sir, the type that always get a laugh?

DIONYSUS: Yes, whatever. But not "I'm feeling crushed". I'm sick of that already.

XANTHIAS: Anything else you would like me to avoid?

DIONYSUS: Yes. Don't say "I'm under pressure" That is just as bad.

XANTHIAS: Oh. I've got a good one!

DIONYSUS: Just get on with it, but don't...

XANTHIAS: Don't what?

DIONYSUS: Don't say anything about needing to "relieve yourself" then farting.

XANTHIAS: Can't I even say that I need a dump?

DIONYSUS: I think I'm going to be sick.

XANTHIAS: Then why am I even carrying this stuff if I don't get to do the lines that you will find in every Greek comedy? There is always a bag carrying routine.

DIONYSUS: Just don't. Whenever I hear one of those baggage routines in the theatre it puts a year on my life.

XANTHIAS: Three times I am knocked back. The weight is on my shoulders, yet I cannot tell a joke.

DIONYSUS: (*To Audience.*) See? This is what happens when you spoil him. Here I am, Dionysus, the son of Flagon, yet I am the one who must toil away on foot whilst he gets to ride on a donkey!

SFX: A Donkey brays. The actors glance over to the direction of the noise.

XANTHIAS: I still have to carry all this.

DIONYSUS: How are you carrying it?

XANTHIAS: Most unwillingly.

DIONYSUS: Would you not say that the donkey is carrying it?

XANTHIAS: For the love of Zeus! No. I am the one doing the carrying.

DIONYSUS: But how can you be carrying something when you are being carried yourself?

XANTHIAS: I don't know. Ask my shoulders.

DIONYSUS: Well, if the donkey is no use to you, why not swap over and carry him instead?

XANTHIAS: Oh, stuff this. If I had fought in that battle at sea I would have been freed from slavery. Then I would be free to tell you to bugger off!

DIONYSUS: Oh, stop your moaning. We are here at our first destination.

HERACLES: (*Off.*) Who is there making all that noise? What in Zeus' name is going on?

DIONYSUS: Slave.

XANTHIAS: Yes.

DIONYSUS: Did you hear?

XANTHIAS: What?

DIONYSUS: How scared he is of me.

XANTHIAS: He is scared that you are a lunatic!

HERACLES: (*Entering laughing. He is dressed in a similar fashion to Dionysus.*) For the love of all the Gods, I cannot stop myself from laughing. I'm biting my lip, but I still cannot stop. (*He laughs.*)

DIONYSUS: Heracles. Please come here. I have a favour to ask.

HERACLES: I'm sorry but it is just too funny. Why in the name of Demeter are you dressed as you are? Where on Earth are you headed?

DIONYSUS: I'll tell you. The thing is, we have been on board ship, sailing with Cleisthenes.

HERACLES: With Cleisthenes, eh. You were fighting?

DIONYSUS: Yes, and we sank more than a dozen of the enemy's ships.

HERACLES: Just the two of you?

DIONYSUS: Just us two.

XANTHIAS: In your dreams.

DIONYSUS: Anyway, whilst on board I was reading The Andromeda and I had a sudden desire, a sudden pang of longing that I could not resist.

HERACLES: (*Looking at Dionysus's groin.*) A pang?

DIONYSUS: Yes.

HERACLES: A big one?

DIONYSUS: No, just a small one

HERACLES: Caused by a woman?

DIONYSUS: No.

HERACLES: A boy?

DIONYSUS: No, no.

HERACLES: A man?

DIONYSUS: Certainly not.

HERACLES: Don't knock it if you haven't tried it. Hey! Was it for Cleisthenes?

DIONYSUS: Don't mock me, brother. This desire has taken hold of me so strongly, I fear that I will die if I am not satisfied.

HERACLES: By Zeus, you are in a bad way. Tell me about it, little brother.

DIONYSUS: It is difficult to describe. Let me try an analogy. Have you ever had a sudden craving for lentil soup?

HERACLES: Lentil soup? Of course. A thousand times.

DIONYSUS: Am I making myself clear? Do you understand, or shall I try a different way?

HERACLES: No, lentil soup I understand, just fine.

DIONYSUS: Well, that is the sort of craving that devours me now, not for soup, but for Euripides.

HERACLES: Euripides?

DIONYSUS: Yes.

HERACLES: The poet?

DIONYSUS: Yes.

HERACLES: The dead poet?

DIONYSUS: No one will persuade me not to follow my desire.

HERACLES: Do you mean below, to the underworld? To hell?

DIONYSUS: And lower still, if there is a lower still.

HERACLES: But why?

DIONYSUS: I crave the writings of a good poet. And all the good ones are dead.

HERACLES: Isn't Iophon still alive?

DIONYSUS: He is about the only decent one left, and I'm not sure he is that good.

HERACLES: If you are going to bring anyone back, why not Sophocles? Last one out, first one back in!

DIONYSUS: I'm interested to see how Iophon manages without his father to guide him. Besides, Sophocles is so laid back he is probably perfectly happy to dwell in the underworld. Euripides is a complete rogue and will jump at the chance to escape.

HERACLES: How about Agathon? Or Xenocles?

DIONYSUS: Not worth the bother.

HERACLES: Pythangelus?

DIONYSUS: Who?

HERACLES: (*Repeating it slowly.*) Pyth-ang-el-us.

DIONYSUS: Can't say I've heard of that one.

The two actors shrug and shake their heads.

XANTHIAS: (*To the audience.*) I might as well not be here. With my shoulders and back so broken. (*He winces to try to elicit sympathy from the audience.*)

HERACLES: But there are thousands of poets still alive, churning out their tragedies faster than Euripides could ever have dreamed.

DIONYSUS: That is true. But they are all crap. A disgrace to their profession. If, by chance, they happen upon a decent idea they muck it up with their incompetence.

They wouldn't recognise creativity if it smacked them round the head.

HERACLES: What do you mean by creativity?

DIONYSUS: Someone who is prepared to be a bit adventurous. Someone who is prepared to take a risk with a phrase like:

A mind that refuses to swear an oath,
But a tongue that has sworn already, never mind the mind.

HERACLES: You like that sort of thing, do you?

DIONYSUS: Like it? I lurve it.

HERACLES: But it is just a load of old bollocks. You must know that.

DIONYSUS: You have your opinion, I have mine.

HERACLES: Utter shite.

DIONYSUS: You are entitled to think what you like, but I didn't come here to seek your view on Euripides.

XANTHIAS: (*To the audience.*) I'm still here, in case you were wondering.

DIONYSUS: I came because I need some travel tips. You ventured down there to rescue Cerberus so you can help me. Where are the ports, the bakeries, the whorehouses? Where might I get a drink or a place to rest my head where there are not too many bedbugs, and the landladies are accommodating?

XANTHIAS: I might as well be invisible.

HERACLES: (*To Xanthias.*) You really want to go along with this?

DIONYSUS: Never mind him, tell me this. Which is the quickest way to Hell? Somewhere not too hot and not too cold.

HERACLES: Well, seeing as you are immortal anyway, the choice is yours really. You could hang yourself?

DIONYSUS: Ooh, no. I don't like the sound of that.

HERACLES: Or I could lend you my pestle and mortar.

DIONYSUS: Hemlock, you mean?

HERACLES: Exactly.

DIONYSUS: No, I couldn't stand that. It sends a deathly chill through the body. I like to keep my tootsies warm.

HERACLES: Oh, I've an idea. There is a place, it is quite close.

DIONYSUS: That's good, I have walked far enough already.

HERACLES: Go down to the pottery in town.

DIONYSUS: Yes

HERACLES: Then climb up that big, tall tower in the centre.

DIONYSUS: Yes, and then what?

HERACLES: Jump off it.

DIONYSUS: What?

HERACLES: Plummet to the ground.

DIONYSUS: No good. That would make mincemeat of my brain.

HERACLES: Then what will you try?

DIONYSUS: The way you went yourself.

HERACLES: But that is a huuuuuggge journey! First you will come to this massive bottomless lake...

DIONYSUS: How do I get across it?

HERACLES: A small boat and an old man. He will row you across for two obols.

DIONYSUS: Aha! The power of two obels.

XANTHIAS: (*To the audience.*) There are six obels in one drachma. You are welcome.

HERACLES: There will be snakes and savage monsters by the thousand.

DIONYSUS: There is no point in trying to scare me. I'm going anyway.

HERACLES: The seas will be filthy, full of sewage and human waste. Turds bobbing in the water like fishing floats. And lying in all this crap you will find anyone who has wronged their house guest, anyone who has robbed a young gigolo, anyone who has smacked their mother or punched their father in the jaw, anyone who has copied out bad poetry...

DIONYSUS: Can we add anything to the list? Anyone who has sang out of key or danced like a sack of chisels perhaps?

HERACLES: But then you will hear the sound of flutes and be bathed in glorious sunshine. All around you will see happy bands of men and women smiling and clapping as they play in the myrtle groves.

DIONYSUS: Who are they?

HERACLES: They are the joyful initiates of the mysteries.

XANTHIAS: The only mystery is why I am the donkey in all of this. I've had enough.

HERACLES: They will tell you everything you need to know, and they live on the very road that you will need to travel. They will lead you directly to the gates of hell where Pluto awaits. Happy travels, my brother. Be lucky.

DIONYSUS: You too.

HERACLES exits.

DIONYSUS: (*To XANTHIAS.*) Now then. Pick up the bags.

XANTHIAS: Like I ever put them down.

DIONYSUS: Just get on with it.

XANTHIAS: Please, I beg you. Hire one of the corpses they are taking for burial. They are going our way, after all.

DIONYSUS: What if I can't find one?

XANTHIAS: I'll just have to manage, but please try.

DIONYSUS: Oh look. There is one now. Hey. Hey you. Yes you, the stiff. Come here. (*CORPSE enters.*). Can you carry this luggage down to the underworld for us?

CORPSE: How many pieces?

DIONYSUS: Just these.

CORPSE: Two drachmas.

DIONYSUS: Two drachmas!

XANTHIAS: Twelve obels!

DIONYSUS: That's too much.

CORPSE: Your choice. (*He goes to leave.*)

DIONYSUS: Wait. Perhaps we can come to some arrangement.

CORPSE: If you are not willing to pay me two drachmas, we have nothing to discuss.

DIONYSUS: What about nine obels?

CORPSE: Two drachmas or no deal, may God strike me, um, alive. Have a nice day.

CORPSE exits.

XANTHIAS: Sanctimonious prick. I'll carry the luggage myself.

DIONYSUS: Good man. To the ferry! (*They exit.*)

SCENE TWO

No one is on stage.

CHARON: (*Off.*) Ahoy! Bring her alongside.

XANTHIAS and DIONYSUS enter.

XANTHIAS: Where are we?

DIONYSUS: This is the lake. The one that Heracles told us about. And look. There is the ferry!

XANTHIAS: Holy Poseidon, yes! And there is the old ferryman, it is Charon.

DIONYSUS: Hey Charon. Charon! Over here.

CHARON: (*Entering.*) All aboard for Troubles End and End of Strife. Anyone for Hell and Damnation?

DIONYSUS: Yes, me.

CHARON: Climb aboard, then.

DIONYSUS: You really go to Hell?

CHARON: Yes, at your service. On you get.

DIONYSUS: (*To XANTHIAS.*) This is us.

CHARON: A slave? I don't take slaves. Not unless they fought in that great battle at sea.

XANTHIAS: Yes, well. I would have done, but I had a bit of an eye infection at the time, you see.

CHARON: Then you must walk round.

XANTHIAS: Oh, very well. Where will I see you?

CHARON: The ferry stop, by the Withering Stone.

DIONYSUS: You understand what you must do?

XANTHIAS: Too well. What have I done to deserve this? (*He exits.*)

CHARON: (*To DIONYSUS*) Sit to the oar.

DIONYSUS sits. CHARON walks about picking on members of the audience at random.

CHARON: Anyone else for the ferry? Would you like to go to Hell, madam? How about you, sir, are you headed for eternal damnation? Hurry, hurry.

He returns to DIONYSUS.

CHARON: What do you think you are doing?

DIONYSUS: What am I doing? Sitting on the oar, like you told me.

CHARON: Not on the oar, bird brain. Sit there!

DIONYSUS: (*Shifting back.*) Here?

CHARON: Now stretch your arms out.

DIONYSUS: Like this?

CHARON: Now plant your feet and...

DIONYSUS: And?

CHARON: Pull.

DIONYSUS: Pull? I cannot row, I don't know how.

CHARON: You will learn quick enough. Dip the oar in the water and you will hear the sweetest melody to keep you in time.

DIONYSUS: A melody? Where does it come from?

CHARON: From the frogs, a most wonderful sound.

DIONYSUS: Very well, give the word.

CHARON: Heave ho! Heave ho!

FROGS:

Bre-ke-ke-ke-kex, co-ax, co-ax,
Bre-ke-ke-ke-kex, co-ax,
Bre-ke-ke-ke-kex, co-ax, co-ax,
Bre-ke-ke-ke-kex, co-ax,
Bre-ke-ke-kex, co-a-ax,
Bre-ke-ke-ke-kex co-ax,
We, the sacred children of the lake,
Let us sing our tuneful song,
And let the rhythm be so very well timed,
That it helps you to row along,
Bre-ke-ke-kex, co-ax, co-ax,
That it helps you to row along.

DIONYSUS: My arse is hurting, this seat is so hard.

FROGS: Bre-ke-ke-ke-kex, co-ax, co-ax. Bre-ke-ke-ke-kex, co-ax.

DIONYSUS: Not that you care.

FROGS: Bre-ke-ke-ke-kex, co-ax, co-ax. Bre-ke-ke-ke-kex, co-ax.

DIONYSUS: To hell with you and your co-ax, you are nothing but co-ax.

FROGS:

Bre-ke-ke-ke-kex, co-ax, co-ax,
Bre-ke-ke-ke-kex, co-ax,
Bre-ke-ke-ke-kex, co-ax, co-ax,
Bre-ke-ke-ke-kex, co-ax,
Bre-ke-ke-kex, co-a-ax,
Bre-ke-ke-ke-kex co-ax,
Mind your own business, big head,
We are loved by one and all,
The horn-footed Pan who plays his pipe,
Always answers to our call,
Bre-ke-ke-kex, co-ax, co-ax,
Always answers to our call.

DIONYSUS: My hands are blistered, and my arse is red raw. I fear I will shit myself at any moment.

FROGS: Bre-ke-ke-ke-kex, co-ax, co-ax. Bre-ke-ke-ke-kex, co-ax.

DIONYSUS: You've made your point, enough now.

FROGS: Bre-ke-ke-ke-kex, co-ax, co-ax. Bre-ke-ke-ke-kex, co-ax.

DIONYSUS: Give it a rest, will you please?

Bre-ke-ke-ke-kex, co-ax, co-ax,
Bre-ke-ke-ke-kex, co-ax,
Bre-ke-ke-ke-kex, co-ax, co-ax,
Bre-ke-ke-ke-kex, co-ax,
Bre-ke-ke-kex, co-a-ax,
Bre-ke-ke-ke-kex co-ax,
Now we will sing even louder still,
Remembering the days of sun,
When we danced our way through the marshes,
The festival has begun,
Bre-ke-ke-kex, co-ax, co-ax,
The festival has begun.

FROGS: and **DIONYSUS:** Bre-ke-ke-ke-kex, co-ax, co-ax. Bre-ke-ke-ke-kex, co-ax.

DIONYSUS: I am taking this song away from you.

FROGS: That is a dreadful thing to do.

DIONYSUS: Not as dreadful as rowing until I burst.

FROGS: and **DIONYSUS:** Bre-ke-ke-ke-kex, co-ax, co-ax. Bre-ke-ke-ke-kex, co-ax.

DIONYSUS: Oh, wail away, see if I care.

FROGS: We'll croak the whole day through.

FROGS: and **DIONYSUS:** Bre-ke-ke-kex, co-a-ax,

DIONYSUS: You won't win at this; I'll see to that.

FROGS: You will not beat us, not a chance.

DIONYSUS: Bre-ke-ke-ke-kex co-ax,

CHARON: Stop! Stop! We have reached the shore. Pay me your fare and we are done.

DIONYSUS stands and hands CHARON some coins.

DIONYSUS: Here are your two obols. Now to find Xanthias.

SCENE THREE

DIONYSUS is alone on stage.

DIONYSUS: Xanthias! Are you here?

XANTHIAS: (*Off.*) Yoohoo!

DIONYSUS: Come here.

XANTHIAS: (*Entering.*) Here I am, master.

DIONYSUS: What have you seen?

XANTHIAS: Mostly filth and darkness.

DIONYSUS: Did you see the rogues that Heracles described? The oath breakers and charlatans?

XANTHIAS: Did you?

DIONYSUS: (*Looking at the audience.*) I see them still.

XANTHIAS: Best we get a move on. This is where Heracles said we would encounter monsters.

DIONYSUS: Nonsense. He was just making it all up to try to scare me. He is jealous of what a good fighter I am, so made up a load of rubbish to make himself look good. Do you know what, I hope I do encounter something. That way I will have a tale to tell.

XANTHIAS: Hush. I hear a noise.

DIONYSUS: Where?

XANTHIAS: It is behind us.

DIONYSUS: Get behind me. (*He does.*)

XANTHIAS: No, it's in front.

DIONYSUS: Get in front of me. (*He does.*)

XANTHIAS: I see it. A most ferocious monster!

DIONYSUS: What is it like?

XANTHIAS: It keeps changing. First it is a bull, then it is a mule.

DIONYSUS: The foul beast.

XANTHIAS: Now it is a girl. The prettiest girl I ever saw.

DIONYSUS: (*Emerging.*) Where is she?

XANTHIAS: Now it's a dog.

DIONYSUS: (*Diving back behind XANTHIAS.*) What sort of shapeshifter is this?

XANTHIAS: Its face is ablaze with fire.

DIONYSUS: Has it a copper leg?

XANTHIAS: Yes! And one made of dung.

DIONYSUS: Where shall I run?

XANTHIAS: Where shall I?

DIONYSUS: (*walking over to the audience.*) Someone save us. I'll buy you a drink!

XANTHIAS: For the love of Heracles, we're done for.

DIONYSUS: Don't use that name.

XANTHIAS: Dionysus, then.

DIONYSUS: That's worse!

XANTHIAS: (*To the shapeshifter.*) Begone. Leave us. Retreat. Depart. On your way, son. (*To DIONYSUS.*) Master.

DIONYSUS: (*Fearful.*) What is it now?

XANTHIAS: We are safe. After the storm comes the calm. The shapeshifter is gone.

DIONYSUS: Do you swear?

XANTHIAS: I swear by Zeus.

DIONYSUS: Swear again.

XANTHIAS: By Zeus.

DIONYSUS: Again.

XANTHIAS: By Zeusy, weusy, deusy.

DIONYSUS: Oh Lord, how pale I was.

XANTHIAS: Your trousers have turned brown with fright.

DIONYSUS: Which God is to blame for my undoing?

XANTHIAS: A tongue that has sworn already, never mind the mind.

DIONYSUS: Hush!

SFX: Flute music.

XANTHIAS: What's the matter.

DIONYSUS: Do you hear it?

XANTHIAS: What?

DIONYSUS: The breath of flutes.

XANTHIAS: I hear it. Do you smell the torches?

DIONYSUS: Let us crouch down and listen. (*They do.*)

CHORUS: (*Off.*)

Oh Iacchus! Oh Iacchus! Oh!
Oh Iacchus! Oh Iacchus! Oh!

XANTHIAS: Master! It is the joyful initiates of the mysteries that Heracles told you about. Singing that song to Iacchus we hear so often.

DIONYSUS: I think you are right. But let's keep quiet until we are certain.

The CHORUS enters.

CHORUS:

Oh Iacchus, honoured God,
This is your home and place of rest,
Come join your sacred band and dance,
The dance that you do best.

XANTHIAS: Holy daughter of Demeter, they are offering a piglet as a sacrifice. Oh, that sweet smell of roast pork.

DIONYSUS: Keep your patience, there might be some crackling going spare.

CHORUS:

Oh Iacchus! Oh Iacchus! Oh!
Oh Iacchus! Oh Iacchus! Oh!

Come to us and raise a torch,
You radiant star of our nocturnal rites,
The meadow is now ablaze with your light,
Emulating day in the middle of the night.

Oh Iacchus! Oh Iacchus! Oh!
Oh Iacchus! Oh Iacchus! Oh!

Old men shake off their years and sorrows,
Troublesome knees are long forgotten,
Iacchus blazing with brilliant light,
Let us forget all that is rotten.

Oh Iacchus! Oh Iacchus! Oh!
Oh Iacchus! Oh Iacchus! Oh!

Step aside impure of thought,
Any stranger to the steps of the dance,
Anyone who knows not the noble muses,
Anyone opposed to romance.

Step aside the immoral politicians who,
On seeing our city destroyed by plague,

Do line their pockets and those of their friends,
Their knowledge of the law quite vague.

Step aside the corrupt officials who,
Turn a blind eye to illegal trade,
So long as they get their five percent,
So long as there's money to be made.

Step aside the pompous celebrity who,
On seeing their name in a play,
Fails to see the funny side,
And insists that the playwright must pay.

Oh Iacchus! Oh Iacchus! Oh!
Oh Iacchus! Oh Iacchus! Oh!

The rest of you start up the singing,
We will dance all through the night and more,
Going forward into the flowery meadows,
Laughing until our lungs are sore.

Also step forward and be sure to raise,
Your voice to our fruitful Queen,
She is the saviour who, through her care,
Performs who duties, unseen.

Demeter, our Queen at our side,
Keep us, your chorus, secure,
And let us play and sing and dance,
And be merry and wholesome and pure.

With your permission I have jokes to tell,
And much to say, sincere,
Your festival can be the excuse we need,
For our inhibitions to all disappear.

Oh Iacchus! Oh Iacchus! Oh!
Oh Iacchus! Oh Iacchus! Oh!

DIONYSUS: I think I'd quite like to join the chorus myself.

XANTHIAS: Me too.

DIONYSUS: (*Approaching the CHORUS.*) Can any of you tell me where is the door to the underworld? We are strangers who have just arrived.

CHORUS:

Then you need to travel no more,
The place you seek is near,
Pluto, Hades or Underworld,
The entrance is right here.

DIONYSUS: Pick up the bags, Slave.

XANTHIAS: Here we go again.

CHORUS:

Oh Iacchus! Oh Iacchus! Oh!
Oh Iacchus! Oh Iacchus! Oh!

Go now through the holy circle,
Skipping through flowery glades,
All who join us in this festival,
Persephone's faithful maids.

Let us go to the rose gardens,
The meadows that blossom with flowers,
We, the initiates of the mysteries,

The pleasure is all ours.

The CHORUS exits.

DIONYSUS: How should I knock, do you think? How do the locals knock, I wonder?

XANTHIAS: Don't waste time thinking about it. You are dressed as Heracles, so act as Heracles.

DIONYSUS: Knock, knock!

AEACUS: Who's there?

DIONYSUS: I, Heracles the strong!

AEACUS: I, Heracles the strong... Oh! It's you, is it? You disgusting, arrogant, brutal man. You are the one that kidnapped my dog, Cerberus, dragged him out and strangled him. Then you ran away taking him with you. But now you are back. The black hearted rocks of Styx and the blood-stained cliffs of Acheron are watching you. The dogs and the hundred-headed viper of Cocytus will rip out your guts. The Tartessian lamprey will lock onto your ribs, and the Tithrasian Gorgons will mangle and tear out your kidneys. I'll just nip and fetch them.

AEACUS exits. DIONYSUS drops to the ground.

XANTHIAS: Ye Gods, what have you done?

DIONYSUS: Well, apart from anything else, I think I have just shat myself.

XANTHIAS: Get up, you fool, before anyone sees you.

DIONYSUS: I feel faint. Have you a cloth? Dab it on my heart.

XANTHIAS: Here. Do it yourself.

XANTHIAS passes DIONYSUS a cloth that he uses to wipe his backside.

XANTHIAS: That's a funny place for your heart.

DIONYSUS: It got frightened and went to hide in my bowels.

XANTHIAS: You are such a coward.

DIONYSUS: I'm not a coward. A coward wouldn't have asked you for a cloth.

XANTHIAS: What are you talking about?

DIONYSUS: A coward would have lain there quivering. I got up and dusted myself down.

XANTHIAS: My mistake. You are quite the hero.

DIONYSUS: Yes, I am. Besides. Were you not frightened by all those threats?

XANTHIAS: Me? No. Didn't bother me.

DIONYSUS: Well then. If you are so brave, let us swap places. You wear the loincloth and carry the club. I'll be the slave and carry the luggage.

XANTHIAS: Very well. (*They swap outer garments.*) You will see that I am no coward.

DIONYSUS: (*Amused by XANTHIAS in the loincloth.*) No. You are just ridiculous.

MAID enters.

MAID: Oh, Heracles, my darling, you have arrived! The Goddess heard you were coming and had some fresh bread baked ready for you. There are two or three pots of lentil soup bubbling away, she has barbecued a whole ox, and made honey cakes. Come in, come in.

XANTHIAS: (*Declining*) No, no. You're too kind.

MAID: But you must. I will not let you go. Why, she's stewing some juicy chicken breasts, preparing a feast of desserts and decanting the finest wines.

XANTHIAS: (*Still declining,*) It all sounds lovely, but...

MAID: Oh, don't be silly. I'm not letting you leave now. There is a girl who plays the pipes so beautifully, and dancing girls, and...

XANTHIAS: Dancing girls?

MAID: Oh yes. Young and freshly plucked.

XANTHIAS: In that case, tell those dancing girls, their master is coming. My slave will bring the bags.

MAID exits.

DIONYSUS: Hold on a second. You didn't take me seriously, did you? I was just fooling. Here, give me back the loincloth and take the bags.

XANTHIAS: What? You intend us to swap back?

DIONYSUS: Intend? I'm doing it. Off with that lionskin.

XANTHIAS: May the Gods be witness to this.

DIONYSUS: Gods indeed! The very thought that you, a slave, a mere mortal, could pass yourself off as Heracles.

XANTHIAS: Here, take the loincloth. You will require my services again soon enough.

SCENE FOUR

DIONYSUS and XANTHIAS change back their outerwear. The CHORUS enters.

CHORUS:

Oh Iacchus! Oh Iacchus! Oh!
Oh Iacchus! Oh Iacchus! Oh!

Praise to anyone who can be decisive,
And can stick to a decision through thick and thin,
But let us admire the crafty stateman,
Who's U-turns get us in a spin.

DIONYSUS: (*Addressing the CHORUS angrily.*) It is laughable to think of him tangled up in the sheets with dancing girls whilst I stand aside and watch. Imagine a punch in the jaw that wipes a smile off the chorus of teeth!

DIONYSUS turns his back, and the CHORUS becomes Innkeepers.

LANDLADY: Plathane! Look. That is the bastard who came into our inn and devoured sixteen loaves of bread.

PLATHANE: You're right. That's him all right.

XANTHIAS: (*To the audience, mimicking the song by Shampoo.*) Uh Oh, he's in trouble.

LANDLADY: And twenty steaks at half an obel each.

XANTHIAS: Something's come along to burst his bubble.

LANDLADY: Plus, all that garlic.

DIONYSUS: I have no idea what you are talking about.

LANDLADY: Did you think I wouldn't recognise you? I haven't even mentioned all that fish you ate.

PLATHANE: Then there's the cheese.

LANDLADY: And just as I was working out the bill he started screaming and shouting.

XANTHIAS: (*To DIONYSUS.*) That does sound like you, to be fair.

LANDLADY: Then he drew his sword and started acting crazy.

PLATHANE: I remember.

LANDLADY: We were so scared we ran upstairs, and he ran off, taking our bedding with him.

XANTHIAS: That is just so like him!

LANDLADY: You monstrous glutton. I could take a rock and smash the teeth that chewed my food.

PLATHANE: And I'd like to throw you into a pit.

LANDLADY: I'd like to take a knife and rip out the throat that swallowed my sausages. I'll fetch a judge and have you in court by the end of the day.

The innkeepers/CHORUS exit.

DIONYSUS: (To XANTHIAS.) Xanthias! May God strike me dead if I don't love you with all my heart.

XANTHIAS: I know what you are thinking, and you can stop it right now. I'm not going to swap again.

DIONYSUS: My dear, darling Xanthias.

XANTHIAS: The very thought that I, a slave, a mere mortal, could pass myself off as Heracles.

DIONYSUS: I know you are angry; you have every right to be. And if you want to punch me, I will not complain. But I promise you, this is the last time. If I ever ask you to swap back again may my wife, my children and myself be destroyed.

XANTHIAS: I didn't know that you were married. Or had any children.

DIONYSUS: Oh yes. Definitely.

XANTHIAS: In that case, I accept.

They swap clothes again. The CHORUS enters.

CHORUS:

Oh Iacchus! Oh Iacchus! Oh!
Oh Iacchus! Oh Iacchus! Oh!

Once again, slave becomes master,
By donning the magnificent atire,
But remember that now you must act like a God,
If you are not to be discovered a liar.

XANTHIAS: (*To the CHORUS.*) Thank you. That had not escaped my notice. What's more, if do we get out of this, he will want the costume back regardless of what he just said, but I will be brave, nonetheless.

AEACUS enters.

AEACUS: (*Addressing the CHORUS.*) Seize this dog napper. Tie him up so that we can give him the punishment he deserves.

DIONYSUS: Oh dear. Look who's back.

XANTHIAS: Stay away from me.

AEACUS: Oh, you fancy a fight, do you? (*To the CHORUS.*) Come on, let's give him a thrashing.

DIONYSUS: How dreadful. This man steals from you then starts a brawl.

AEACUS: Monstrous.

DIONYSUS: Awful. Terrible.

XANTHIAS: By Zeus, If I ever came here before and stole from you, then I am ready to die for it. But let me make you an offer. Take my slave and torture him. Ask him what he knows. If you still find me in the wrong, then you may kill me.

AEACUS: Torture him? How?

XANTHIAS: However you wish. You could tie him to a ladder, hang him, lash him, whip him, flay him, stretch him, pour vinegar up his nostrils, pile hot bricks on him, whatever takes your fancy. Don't hit him with a leek though. That would be silly.

AEACUS: That sounds reasonable. But, if I were to damage your slave in this process, then I would gladly compensate.

XANTHIAS: Oh, there is no need for that. Just take him away and flog him.

AEACUS: I'll do it right here. That way he has to look you in the eye as he speaks. (*To DIONYSUS.*) Now then. Put down those bags and make sure to tell us the truth.

DIONYSUS: I beg you, don't torture me. I am a God. You would regret it for evermore.

AEACUS: Wait. What's that you are saying?

DIONYSUS: I am Dionysus, son of Zeus, I am immortal. He is the slave.

AEACUS: Do you hear him?

XANTHIAS: Oh yes, I hear him all right. Flog him some more, I say. If he is a God, he won't even feel it.

DIONYSUS: Well, since you claim that you are a God, why don't you also get beaten. After all, you won't feel it, yourself.

XANTHIAS: Good point, well made. Then, let this be a test. Whichever one of us flinches or cries out the first, then he is not a God.

AEACUS: You are a gentleman, sir. It is a very fair solution. Strip off, then.

DIONYSUS and XANTHIAS remove their outer garments.

XANTHIAS: How will you ensure that the test is fair?

AEACUS: Easy. You will take it in turns. A blow for you then a blow for him.

XANTHIAS: Excellent. Let's get going then (*AEACUS hits him.*), see if you spot me flinch.

AEACUS: I already hit you.

XANTHIAS: (*Incredulously.*) No! I didn't feel a thing.

AEACUS: Interesting. Let me try the other one. (*He hits DIONYSUS.*)

DIONYSUS: Ready when you are.

AEACUS: I already hit you.

DIONYSUS: You hit me? Then why didn't I notice?

AEACUS: I don't know. I'll try the other one again.

XANTHIAS: Be quick. (*AEACUS hits him.*) Haaaaa!

AEACUS: Haaaaa? Did I hurt you?

XANTHIAS: No, no. I was just thinking Haaaaaw long is it now until the festival of Heracles?

AEACUS: Oh! You are a religious man! Righto, back to the other one. (*He hits DIONYSUS.*)

DIONYSUS: Arrgggh!

AEACUS: What?

DIONYSUS: Um. I can see some men on horseback.

AEACUS: So, why the tears?

DIONYSUS: They are carrying onions.

AEACUS: I see. Nothing else bothering you?

DIONYSUS: (*Cheerfully.*) No, nothing at all.

AEACUS: Back to the first one then. (*He hits XANTHIAS.*)

XANTHIAS: Ah, ah, ah, ah, ah, ah.

AEACUS: What is it?

XANTHIAS: I'm just pulling out a splinter.

AEACUS: This is strange behaviour. Your turn. (*He hits DIONYSUS.*)

DIONYSUS: (*Screaming.*) LORD APOLLO! (*Quietly.*) God of music and poetry.

XANTHIAS: He flinched! You heard him!

DIONYSUS: No, I didn't. I was just remembering a poem by Sophocles.

XANTHIAS: Don't mess about, now. Give him a good old smack in the ribs.

AEACUS: Good idea. Turn this way, please. (*He punches DIONYSUS in the chest.*)

DIONYSUS: (*Screaming.*) LORD GOD, POSEIDON!

XANTHIAS: There!

DIONYSUS: (*Jauntily.*) Noble God of the seas, ruling the Aegean peaks and creeks and over the deep blue main. I always loved that poem.

AEACUS: This is no good. I'm never going to be able to work out which of you is the God. Better that you come inside and let my lord, Pluto, take a look at you. He should be able to tell, being a God himself.

DIONYSUS: Good idea! I wish you had thought of that before you started hitting us!

END OF ACT ONE

ACT TWO

SCENE ONE

CHORUS:

Oh Iacchus! Oh Iacchus! Oh!
Oh Iacchus! Oh Iacchus! Oh!

Welcome back, ladies and gentlemen
The second part is about to begin
You are so wise to choose to return to your seats
And see it right through to the fin. Ish.

CHORUS LEADER: Dear audience. I hope you are refreshed, relieved and ready for more. To those of you who are familiar with Greek drama, this is the Parabasis. The bit of the play when the leader of the chorus, that's me, gets to talk to you directly. First things first, I think it has been going rather well, don't you? If some of it is going over your head, don't worry about that. It is just because you are stupid.

So, a quick recap. Dionysus has decided that all the new poetry sounds the same. It might as well just be noise. Call that writing? In my day, poems were about something. Etcetera. Now, whilst most of us would just dig out the old stuff and ignore the new, Dionysus has a better idea. He will go down to Hell and bring back his pop idol, Euripides, presumably thinking that there is still a place for oldies but goodies on Top of the Acrops.

Being a God, he doesn't go by himself, but takes his slave, Xanthias. You may have noticed that Xanthias is a bit of a character. Truth is, he is not at all happy about being a slave. He has fought in many sea battles but, sadly for him, not the one that counts. Had he fought at Arginusae he would have been freed. Why that one was different, you tell me. It is the same as the refugees from Plataea. They are welcomed with open arms. Come on in, we have plenty of room. But refugees from anywhere else. Not the same story. We don't want you. We don't need you. Get back on the boat. I don't see why all our citizens cannot be treated fairly and equally. Not much to ask, is it?

Anyway, back to the story. Dionysus goes to see his brother, Heracles... Oh actually, hang on. Let's talk about the family tree for a minute. It all starts with Chaos. That is actually the name of the God but believe me, it is no coincidence. Now, Chaos had a son, Erebus, meaning "darkness" and a daughter, Nyx, meaning "night". Yes, I know they sound like they are the same thing, but they are not. Erebus and Nyx had a load of offspring, don't ask, including Aether, meaning "heaven" and Hemera, meaning "day". Now it starts to make sense, right? Skip forward a few generations and you get to Zeus, who put it about a bit to say the least. One of his many conquests was Semele, who gave him a son, the hero of our story, Dionysus. Another conquest was Alcmene, a married woman (naughty) who gave birth to Heracles. All of which means that Dionysus and Heracles were brothers from different mothers. But with the same father.

Heracles had been down to hell previously to fetch that dear little three headed pooch Cerberus. It was a kind of challenge because Heracles is only half God and not immortal, so he was expected to fail, especially as he was told that he was not allowed to use any weapons. Nevertheless, with just a dodgy loincloth for protection, he did fetch back little Cerby, much to the annoyance of everyone concerned. Having presented Cerberus to the king, he was told to let the little doggy return to the underworld, but in return Heracles was released from his twelve labours, but that is a whole different play. However, it does explain why Dionysus didn't get the reception he was hoping for when he got down to Hell himself. Oh, and if you hadn't realised. The God Hades and the God Pluto are the same person but, what with Hell also being called Hades, we use Pluto to avoid confusion. Clear? Good.

Right. I think we are about ready to go again, but just in case you are feeling a bit lost, just remember this. Old good, new bad. That is all this play is about, that is all that any play by Aristophanes is about, if we are being honest. Basically, he liked things to be the way they always had been. Think about the furniture we have in our homes. We treat our furniture the same way that we treat people. A sturdy chair, made to the highest quality and of the finest materials is cast aside and replaced by a cheap imitation. The old languishes in obscurity, rotting away through lack of use, whilst the new provides a few years of less than satisfactory service before completely collapsing. Am I still talking about furniture or the government? (*Pause to let it sink in*) That, ladies and gentlemen, is Greek theatre, in a nutshell. Meanwhile, back in Hell, Xanthias and Aeacus, the doorman we met in act one, are comparing notes.

AEACUS: That master of yours is pretty good to you, isn't he?

XANTHIAS: Why wouldn't he be? All he really cares about is drinking and shagging.

AEACUS: But not to have beaten you for pretending that you were the master and he the slave.

XANTHIAS: He would have been sorry if he had tried it.

AEACUS: You're a man after my own heart.

XANTHIAS: Oh, yes?

AEACUS: It feels so good to curse my Pluto behind his back.

XANTHIAS: Do you like to complain after he has beaten you with a stick?

AEACUS: I certainly do.

XANTHIAS: Do you enjoy snooping on him?

AEACUS: More than anything else.

XANTHIAS: And, Zeus protect us, listening to everything your masters say?

AEACUS: I love it.

XANTHIAS: And passing on the gossip?

AEACUS: I'm in Heaven!

XANTHIAS: In that case, please tell me, what on Earth was all that noise about? All the shouting and abuse?

AEACUS: Oh, that's just Aeschylus and Euripides.

XANTHIAS: Eh?

AEACUS: The corpses are revolting.

XANTHIAS: Why?

AEACUS: It is the custom here that the most accomplished artist in his line of work gets free meals in the main hall and a seat at the top table.

XANTHIAS: I see.

AEACUS: But if another comes along who is more accomplished in the same line of work, then he must give up his place.

XANTHIAS: How does that effect Aeschylus?

AEACUS: He was the one who had that privilege.

XANTHIAS: Who has it now?

AEACUS: When Euripides arrived, he started showing off to all the lowlifes. The villains and muggers, the murderers and thieves – there are quite a few of them down here. His pompous material appealed to the riffraff, and they hailed him a genius. It all went to his head, and he claimed his place at the table.

XANTHIAS: Did Aeschylus get kicked off, then?

AEACUS: No, but the mob went wild. They demanded a trial to see who was best.

XANTHIAS: What, those degenerates?

AEACUS: They raised the roof.

XANTHIAS: Did no one support Aeschylus?

AEACUS: Good taste is a rarity down here (*Regards the audience.*) As it is elsewhere.

XANTHIAS: So, what is going to happen?

AEACUS: There will be a contest. Their skills will be measured and compared.

XANTHIAS: But what about Sophocles? How come he isn't the one at the top table?

AEACUS: Oh, you know Sophocles. Aeschylus offered him his place, but he refused. He is happy to just sit in reserve. But if Euripides wins the contest, then he has vowed to go up against him himself.

XANTHIAS: So, it is really going to go ahead?

AEACUS: Oh, yes. Any moment now. Their poetry will be placed on the scales.

XANTHIAS: What! Like lumps of meat?

AEACUS: They will get out their rulers and set squares...

XANTHIAS: Are they making bricks?

AEACUS: Their wedges and compasses. Euripides said they will be measured word for word.

XANTHIAS: I bet Aeschylus is well pissed.

AEACUS: He's not best pleased.

XANTHIAS: So, who will be the judge?

AEACUS: Well, that's just it. There is a bit of a shortage of connoisseurs of the arts down here, so they have ended up asking your master to judge.

XANTHIAS: Dionysus!

AEACUS: Yes. We had better go in. Should anything go wrong our masters will be looking around for a slave to blame.

SCENE TWO

CHORUS:

Oh Iacchus! Oh Iacchus! Oh!
Oh Iacchus! Oh Iacchus! Oh!

The time has come for the greatest challenge,
Soon we will know which one is the best,
Let's hope we don't hear that golden buzzer,
Hades has talent, let us begin our quest.

PLUTO: Well, Dionysus, Are you ready?

DIONYSUS: As ready as I will ever be, Pluto.

PLUTO: In which case I will stand back and spectate.

EURIPIDES: Let me just make this clear. I'm going nowhere. I am the GOAT.

DIONYSUS: GOAT?

EURIPIDES: Greatest Of All Time.

DIONYSUS: Well, Aeschylus? What do you say to that?

EURIPIDES: Oh, he will start with a grand opening, gesticulating wildly, just like his tragedies.

DIONYSUS: Now, now. Don't get cocky.

EURIPIDES: I saw through him long ago. His crude, rambling, pretentious, and long-winded verses don't fool me.

AESCHYLUS: Hah! Says you, a man whose greatest asset is the ability to gather gossip. You are nothing but an embarrassment. You will regret your words.

DIONYSUS: Steady on, Aeschylus, don't lose your shit just yet.

AESCHYLUS: I won't stop until I have exposed this corny merchant for what he is.

DIONYSUS: Batten down the hatches, boys, the storm is about to burst.

AESCHYLUS: Nothing but a thief of those who went before him. Not one original thought in his head.

DIONYSUS: Aeschylus, please control yourself. Euripides, you had best take cover in case this onslaught batters you into pontification. Now then, Aeschylus. Let us have a civilised debate. This is not Mykonos on a Saturday night. You explode into flames like an oak struck by lightning.

EURIPIDES: I can handle him. If dog eat dog is what he wants, then dog eat dog is what he will get. Whether it is my diction, my songs, or the very fibre of my work he will not get the better of me.

DIONYSUS: How do you propose we settle this, Aeschylus?

AESCHYLUS: Well, I would have preferred not to have held the contest here, where we cannot be judged on equal terms.

DIONYSUS: What do you mean by that?

AESCHYLUS: I mean that my work has not died with me. The citizens still recall with pleasure some of my cherished text. Every word he said is all but forgotten. Nevertheless, we must do what we must do.

DIONYSUS: Very well. Someone bring incense so that I may pray that my judgement is sound. (*To the Chorus*) Please begin.

Opening Prayers

Incense is lit and the smell reaches the audience.

CHORUS:

Oh Iacchus! Oh Iacchus! Oh!
Oh Iacchus! Oh Iacchus! Oh!

Let us pray to the holy maidens of Zeus,
That this contest is honourable and fair,
That the contestants don't fail to find the right word,
Oh, Great Lord Zeus, hear our prayer.

DIONYSUS: Ready, you two? Now, say your prayers.

AESCHYLUS: Oh Demeter, my mistress, who nourishes of my soul, make me worthy of your love.

DIONYSUS: (*To Euripides*) Your turn.

EURIPIDES: Thank you, but I pray to a different deity.

DIONYSUS: You have your own Gods?

EURIPIDES: Precisely.

DIONYSUS: Very well, pray to them.

EURIPIDES: (*Pompously*) Might I, through my own intellect, wit and way with words, win this argument and put him straight.

Prelude

CHORUS:

Oh Iacchus! Oh Iacchus! Oh!
Oh Iacchus! Oh Iacchus! Oh!

The stage is ready, the poets too,
Their words will form a merry dance,
A war of words is what we'll endure,
Nothing is left to chance.

One will wield with artistic skill,
Clever wordplay and wit refined,
The other, will show with defiant words,
he has left the other behind.

Round One

CHORUS LEADER: Round one. Style.

DIONYSUS: Gentlemen, begin. No cliches, no metaphors, nothing that any old fool might say.

EURIPIDES: Right then! I will discuss my own body of work when I get to my closing remarks, but first let me deliberate on this, my rival. This pretentious quack, charlatan, and cheat. I will show how he has deceived his audience, treating them as fools so that he might seem superior by comparison. He would sit his characters down and cover their faces with masks and they would make not a sound. Not even a grunt.

DIONYSUS: He's right. Not a grunt.

EURIPIDES: Then the choruses would belt out song after song, but the actors remained silent.

DIONYSUS: I quite enjoyed the silences.

EURIPIDES: Then you were an idiot. But I'm sure you realise that now.

DIONYSUS: Oh. Yes, of course. Um. How do you mean?

EURIPIDES: It is a demonstration of what a quack he is. To make us sit there waiting for the actors to speak. The drama would go on and on and on and on.

DIONYSUS: You're right! He took us all in! (*To Aeschylus*) You seem a little uncomfortable.

EURIPIDES: It is because I am exposing him. Then, once we were halfway through, his actor would finally utter dozen words, totally incomprehensible, yet terrifying to behold.

AESCHYLUS: (*Sarcastically.*) Alas I am undone.

DIONYSUS: (*To Aeschylus.*) Oh, be quiet.

EURIPIDES: Not a single word was clear.

DIONYSUS: (*To Aeschylus.*) And stop gnashing your teeth.

EURIPIDES: It was all hooked beak eagles and mattocks, blazons of beaten bronze and horse-crags. Utter nonsense.

DIONYSUS: Oh, yes. I was once kept awake all night wondering what a yellow cockhorse was.

AESCHYLUS: A mascot on a ship you idiot!

DIONYSUS: And there I was thinking it was a dildo.

EURIPIDES: Are cocks really suitable for family entertainment?

AESCHYLUS: And what exactly do you call family entertainment?

EURIPIDES: Well, no cockhorses for a start. And no goat-stags, whatever they are. When I took your place, I found that the genre had become bloated. Stuffed with complicated structures and impenetrable discourse. I stuck it on a diet. I stripped it back and got rid of the padding. The first person on stage would immediately explain the background.

AESCHYLUS: Easier to explain than yours.

EURIPIDES: From the opening words, no character was idle. Slaves, women, the young, the old. Each would speak as much as their masters.

AESCHYLUS: Outrageous! How did you get away with such behaviour?

EURIPIDES: They loved it. It was democratic.

DIONYSUS: You should move on. I don't find this very praiseworthy.

EURIPIDES: Next, I taught people to speak freely.

AESCHYLUS: They did that, all right.

EURIPIDES: I taught them how to think, how to see, to understand, to twist and turn and to love those crafty moves. How to look out for trouble and stay one step ahead.

AESCHYLUS: I don't deny it.

EURIPIDES: I showed them common scenarios understood by all. Things that they could relate to themselves, that seemed familiar. I never strayed into the obscure or confused them with convoluted stories. You can tell us apart by our supporters. His are bearded intellectuals who sit alone and smile, mine are sociable hordes who laugh out loud.

DIONYSUS: I enjoy a good night out, myself.

EURIPIDES: I showed them all how things should be, so that they could look at their own lives see where they have gone wrong. I gave them the knowledge to deduce what was right and what was wrong.

DIONYSUS: That's right! Men go home newly liberated and cry "who moved my slippers?", "where is my favourite cup?" and "who has eaten all the tit bits?" No longer are they meek and silent.

CHORUS:

Oh Iacchus! Oh Iacchus! Oh!
Oh Iacchus! Oh Iacchus! Oh!

Aeschylus it is your turn to speak,
What have you to say in reply,
Please keep control of that temper of yours,
Don't let it all go awry.

DIONYSUS: Yes, let us hear what you have to say.

AESCHYLUS: It makes me angry that I am even required to respond but let me ask this. What is our purpose? Why should one admire a poet?

EURIPIDES: For his cleverness and good advice. Because we improve the lives of the townsfolk.

AESCHYLUS: So, if you have done the reverse, taken an honest and noble man and turned him into a rogue, what should be your punishment?

DIONYSUS: I can answer that. He deserves to die.

AESCHYLUS: Think of the citizens he inherited from me. Were they not wise, hardworking, and good. Not at all like the lazy, uncouth layabouts we see everywhere today?

All cast survey the audience.

DIONYSUS: Oh dear, he does have a point.

EURIPIDES: So how exactly did you make the citizens wise, hardworking, and good?

DIONYSUS: Yes, Aeschylus, how did you manage that?

AESCHYLUS: Well, my plays were full of war.

DIONYSUS: How does that help?

AESCHYLUS: Men were filled with passion. A desire to fight.

DIONYSUS: Not necessarily a good thing. Doesn't it depend on who they want to fight with?

AESCHYLUS: All good training. I gave people a yearning for an enemy to defeat. Think about what our most noble of poets have given us. Orpheus first revealed the underworld and taught us not to commit murder. Musaeus gave us cure for diseases. Hesiod taught us how to work the soil and understand the seasons whilst Homer, the greatest of them all, taught us courage and how to make the best use of weaponry.

DIONYSUS: That's true. So long as you have the skills to go with the knowledge.

AESCHYLUS: And this was my motivation. Inspired by Homer, I too have created many models of virtue. Men that our citizens will want to emulate when they hear the trumpet call. And with no distractions. No comely wenches to interfere the purpose. There is nothing erotic about the women I have created.

EURIPIDES: God, no. Never a hint of sex.

AESCHYLUS: I should hope note. Whereas your plays are full of it. Wasn't that your downfall?

DIONYSUS: (*To EURIPIDES.*) Oh, yes. The descriptions concerning the pursuit of other men's wives had repercussions close to home, as I recall.

EURIPIDES: (*To AESCHYLUS.*) My only censor is you. What harm comes from a bit of happy frolicking?

AESCHYLUS: Man and wife have separated, having followed your example.

EURIPIDES: Just a minute. I didn't invent adultery.

AESCHYLUS: True, but you made it seem commonplace. It is our responsibility to promote clean living and keep the unsavoury hidden. Children have teachers to show them how to behave, adults rely on us. We have an obligation to encourage good behaviour.

EURIPIDES: So, when you speak on such a grand scale, does that encourage good behaviour? You should speak in plain language if you want your point to be understood.

AESCHYLUS: No, you fool! My point is made with subtlety. Great ideas must be delivered with great words. Besides, the Gods are expected to speak on a higher level, just as they are expected to dress more magnificently than us. At least, that is, until you come along and destroy everything.

EURIPIDES: How?

AESCHYLUS: Firstly, you dress your Kings in rags to make them seem pitiable.

EURIPIDES: And where is the harm, I should like to know?

AESCHYLUS: It is why none of our wealthy citizens are now prepared to sponsor the building of a ship. They wrap themselves in rags and claim to be poor.

DIONYSUS: My God, yes. Whilst underneath they have a nice woolly fleece.

AESCHYLUS: Secondly, you have taught people to be idle. They sit around and chatter. Young men wear out their arses, gossiping and neglecting their duties. The men on a ship now answer back to their superiors; when I was alive all they knew was how to shout heave-ho.

DIONYSUS: And fart in the face of the rower behind, follow through and steal a change of clothes when they reach shore. But now they refuse to row at all, respect for their masters has evaporated.

AESCHYLUS: Is there anything we cannot blame him for? Are there any of society's ills where he is not the creator? Hordes of drunken young men roam the streets at night looking for trouble and usually finding it. Women offer themselves up to whoever will give them some attention, only to find themselves discarded in the morning. Children swear and curse. Our cities are swarming with lowly clerks more versed in horseplay than finance. Our young men are so unfit they can barely lift a torch never mind carry it.

DIONYSUS: By Zeus, you are right. I went to see the games at the Parthenon and the carrier of the torch was so fat, the steps wobbled as he plodded by. He lumbered on, head down and sweating whilst the locals jeered and laughed at him. I laughed myself when, before reaching the centre, he collapsed and farted with such force it blew out the torch. What has become of us?

CHORUS:

Oh Iacchus! Oh Iacchus! Oh!
Oh Iacchus! Oh Iacchus! Oh!

A mighty battle, a violent clash,
It's hard for anyone to choose,
When one has made a forceful point,
The other strives to confuse.

The two of you, there is no time to rest,
there are a lot more attacks to be made,
Make use of any trick you can find,
So that Dionysus is finally swayed.

Round Two

CHORUS LEADER: Round Two. The prologue.

EURIPIDES: Well now. Let me consider your prologues. What better place to start than at the beginning. Let us see how this brilliant writer opens proceedings. We will test the quality that he is so assured of.

DIONYSUS: How will you test this?

EURIPIDES: A number of ways but let us start with the prologue from Oresteia.

DIONYSUS: Right, quiet everyone. Aeschylus, begin.

AESCHYLUS:

Earth born Hermes, watching over a father's realm.
Be my saviour and ally, I beseech you,
For I have come to this land and returned.

DIONYSUS: Any fault there?

EURIPIDES: Where shall I start?

DIONYSUS: But it is just three lines.

EURIPIDES: Each of them horrendous.

DIONYSUS: Perhaps you had better keep silent, Aeschylus, if just three lines can cause such complaint.

AESCHYLUS: Silent for him!

DIONYSUS: That's my advice.

EURIPIDES: He starts with a monstrous error.

AESCHYLUS: Nonsense! Oh, what do I care, let's play along with it. What is my error?

EURIPIDES: Begin the lines again.

AESCHYLUS: Earth born Hermes, watching over a father's realm.

EURIPIDES: Is this line not spoken at the tomb of his dead father?

AESCHYLUS: I don't deny it.

EURIPIDES: Watching over his father as he died a violent death at the hand of his own wife

AESCHYLUS: No. The son had taken over the role of his father.

EURIPIDES: That's even worse.

DIONYSUS: So, his dad taught him how to rob graves?

AESCHYLUS: I think your wine must be off, it is affecting your judgment.

DIONYSUS: Try another line.

AESCHYLUS: Be my saviour and ally, I beseech you, for I have come to this land and returned.

EURIPIDES: Aha!

DIONYSUS: Aha?

EURIPIDES: Yes indeed, Aha.

DIONYSUS: Why Aha?

EURIPIDES: Because he has made a silly mistake. This brilliant and witty genius has just shown himself to be a fool.

DIONYSUS: I don't get it. Say it again.

AESCHYLUS: Be my saviour and ally, I beseech you, for I have come to this land and returned.

EURIPIDES: Do you see? The brilliant Aeschlyus has told us the same thing twice.

DIONYSUS: What do you mean, twice?

EURIPIDES: Well, let me explain. He says, "I have come to this land" but "I have come" means exactly the same as "I returned".

DIONYSUS: So it is. It is like saying, pass me a dish, pass me a bowl.

AESCHYLUS: They are not the same you pumped up windbag. It is an excellent choice of words.

DIONYSUS: What do you mean? They sound the same to me.

AESCHYLUS: Anyone can "come" to a land. Whether you are a first-time visitor or a frequent traveller, anyone can come and go. But a man who has been in exile has both come and returned.

DIONYSUS: I get it. He has come to return to his homeland. That's good. I like it. What do you say, Euripides?

EURIPIDES: I say it is utter bollocks. Never mind. Let us try another line.

AESCHYLUS:

And on this burial mound,
I cry out to my father to hear, to listen.

EURIPIDES: There it is again! He said the same thing twice. (*To the audience.*) You heard him.

DIONYSUS: To be fair, he was talking to the dead. It can take a few goes before you get through to them. Anyway, let us have a look at you. How do you start your prologues?

EURIPIDES: Well, I will tell you this much. If you hear me say the same thing twice you can spit on me.

DIONYSUS: Lovely, I will bear that in mind. Come on then. Let us hear these perfectly tuned prologues of yours.

EURIPIDES:

Oedipus was, at first, a lucky man.

AESCHYLUS: No, he wasn't. Before he was even conceived it was predicted that he's kill his own father. The very definition of born unlucky.

EURIPIDES:

He then became most wretched.

AESCHYLUS: Became? He was never anything else. They tried to keep him in a pot to prevent him from murdering his father and when he grew up, he ended up marrying an old woman who turned out to be his own mother.

EURIPIDES: You are talking nonsense. Each line of my prologues is perfectly crafted.

AESCHYLUS: Oh, I have no need to pick apart your prologues line by line. I can do it quite easily with a little bottle of olive oil.

EURIPIDES: A bottle of oil?

AESCHYLUS: Yes, just the one. Your writing is so monotonous that one will fit all your scenarios. A little blanket, a little baggage, a little bottle. Go ahead, I'll show you.

EURIPIDES: You'll show me?

AESCHYLUS: I will.

DIONYSUS: Very well, begin.

EURIPIDES:

Aegyptus, so the story goes, sailed to Argon where he...

AESCHYLUS: Lost his little bottle.

EURIPIDES: Hold on. What are you talking about? What little bottle?

DIONYSUS: Never mind that. Try another one.

EURIPIDES:

Apollo leapt and danced amid the torches and...

AESCHYLUS: Lost his little bottle.

DIONYSUS: The little bottle has foiled you again.

EURIPIDES: Well, let him try to tack his little bottle onto this one.

There is no man who is blessed in everything.
Either he's lost the will to live or he's

AESCHYLUS: Lost his little bottle.

EURIPIDES: Damn you!

DIONYSUS: I think you had better try some more. This little bottle could be your undoing.

EURIPIDES:

Cadmus had barely left when suddenly he...

AESCHYLUS: Lost his little bottle.

EURIPIDES:

Pelops, with horses, swift

AESCHYLUS: Lost his little bottle.

EURIPIDES:

Oenus from his land set out and...

AESCHYLUS: Lost his little bottle.

DIONYSUS: I'm starting to enjoy this.

EURIPIDES: Please allow me to complete the verse.

Oenus from his land set out and
With corn aplenty for his sacrifice
In the act of honouring the gods
He...

AESCHYLUS & DIONYSUS: Lost his little bottle.

EURIPIDES: You keep out of it. Let him try this.

Zeus, who has been spoken of in truth, has...

AESCHYLUS, DIONYSUS & CHORUS: Lost his little bottle.

For the next three AESCHYLUS encourages the audience to join in.

EURIPIDES:

Semele found out the grape's rich juice, and...

ALL: Lost his little bottle.

EURIPIDES:

When Jove had snatched him from the lightning fire,
He...

ALL: Lost his little bottle.

EURIPIDES:

And when the god came down in all his power,
He...

ALL: Lost his little bottle.

DIONYSUS: Admit is, Euripides. This battle is lost. He will stick that little bottle of his wherever there is room.

EURIPIDES: Oh, bollocks to the stupid prologues. I will beat him in the next round, don't you worry about that!

CHORUS:

Oh Iacchus! Oh Iacchus! Oh!
Oh Iacchus! Oh Iacchus! Oh!

Euripides has his back to the wall,
Two rounds down and two to go,
And next we have the battle of the song,
Our expectations are becoming low.

Round Three

CHORUS LEADER: Round Three. Songs.

EURIPIDES: This is where I will triumph. He claims that my prologues are monotonous, but I can show that all his songs are so repetitive they could be condensed into single verse.

DIONYSUS: I'll take some pebbles and count.

EURIPIDES: Let us start with one of his songs.

Oh, Achilles, you glorious king,
Hear your enemy shout,
Prepare, ye, for the assault,
Prepare, ye, for the assault.

DIONYSUS: That's two assaults already!

EURIPIDES:

Son of the Gods,
That rule the nations,
Listen to what I say,
Prepare, ye, for the assault.

DIONYSUS: A third assault, better watch yourself, Aeschylus.

EURIPIDES:

Keep silent whilst they open the temple,
Prepare, ye, for the assault,
The warriors leave in good heart,
Prepare, ye, for the assault.

DIONYSUS: All these assaults, my kidneys cannot take any more. I think I need the bathroom.

EURIPIDES: Let's have another of his first.

Two powerful monarchs, who reign supreme
Phlattothratto phlattothrat,
Sent the queen, that omen of death,
Phlattothratto phlattothrat.
With an avenging arm, bearing a spear,
Phlattothratto phlattothrat,
To scoop Ajax into the clouds,
Phlattothratto phlattothrat.

DIONYSUS: What on earth is this phlattothratto? Is it a sporting chant or have you stolen it from some sailor's shanty?

AESCHYLUS: Neither. I took them from a fine source and with good cause, so that I could not be accused of harvesting the sacred meadow of the muses. He, on the other hand, happily borrows anything from brothel ballads to romantic love songs. Let me give you an example his.

Halcyons who twitter,
Beside the sea,

Your skin is moist,
From the damp dew.

Long fingered spiders,
under the eves,
We-e-e-eve your web,
In time to the tune.

Music loving dolphins,
Who leap in the dark,
Do you predict,
A favourable voyage?

Grapes on the vine,
Clustered so tight,
Throw out your arms,
And embrace me.

EURIPIDES: A competent if somewhat dispassionate performance.

AESCHYLUS: Well?

DIONYSUS: Well, what?

AESCHYLUS: Did you notice the plodding rhythm?

DIONYSUS: Now that you mention it.

AESCHYLUS: (*To EURIPIDES.*) And you dare to criticise my songs when yours are just the same as can be heard in every whorehouse in Athens?

DIONYSUS: I've had enough of your songs, both of you.

AESCHYLUS: Me too. Let's use the scales at last. These alone can test our poetry. It is the weight of our phrases that will prove who is best.

DIONYSUS: It comes down to this. I must weigh up the skill of these two poets like I was selling cheese.

CHORUS:

Oh Iacchus! Oh Iacchus! Oh!
Oh Iacchus! Oh Iacchus! Oh!

It's not easy being clever
But this sure is a surprise
Weighing words upon a scale
To decide who wins the prize

Round Four

CHORUS LEADER: Round Four. The scales.

DIONYSUS: Right then, each of you stand by your scale.

Members of the CHORUS form a human scale each holding out a pan.

AESCHYLUS and EURIPIDES: We're here.

DIONYSUS: Now hold it whilst you say you line and don't let go until I say cock-a-doodle-doo.

AESCHYLUS and EURIPIDES take hold of a pan each.

AESCHYLUS and EURIPIDES: Ready!

DIONYSUS: Now speak your lines into the pan.

EURIPIDES: Oh, that the ship, Argo, had not flown on its winged way.

AESCHYLUS: River Spercheius, where the cattle graze.

DIONYSUS: Cock-a-doodle-doo!

AESCHYLUS and EURIPIDES let go of their pans. AESCHYLUS's pan drops lower.

DIONYSUS: (*To EURIPIDES.*) His pan has sunk much lower.

EURIPIDES: How come?

DIONYSUS: Because he had a river in his and everything is heavier when it is wet. Yours had wings, for God's sake. How was that ever going to win?

EURIPIDES: Let me try another one.

DIONYSUS: Hold your pans.

AESCHYLUS and EURIPIDES take hold of a pan each.

AESCHYLUS: EURIPIDES: We're ready.

DIONYSUS: Speak your lines.

EURIPIDES: Persuasion has no temple other than reason.

AESCHYLUS: Death is the only one of the Gods that doesn't require gifts.

DIONYSUS: Cock-a-doodle-doo!

AESCHYLUS and EURIPIDES let go of their pans. AESCHYLUS's pan drops lower.

DIONYSUS: Down his scale goes again. That's because he threw in Death this time. The heaviest of all ills.

EURIPIDES: But I used the word persuasion. A champion word if ever there was one.

DIONYSUS: Persuasion is insubstantial. It is nothing on its own. It was never going to beat Death. Choose something big and powerful to weigh down your pan.

EURIPIDES: Let's see. What do I have?

DIONYSUS: I've got one for you. "Achilles cast his dice and threw two ones and a four." Use that one.

EURIPIDES: Very funny. (*With a straight face and spoken deadpan.*) I can barely stop laughing.

DIONYSUS: Come on then. Last go. You will need a big victory in this one, Euripides, if you are going to win this round.

AESCHYLUS and EURIPIDES take hold of a pan each.

AESCHYLUS: EURIPIDES: We're ready.

DIONYSUS: Speak!

EURIPIDES: In his right hand he took a club, weighted with iron.

AESCHYLUS: Chariot on chariot, corpse on corpse.

DIONYSUS: Well, cock-a-bloody-doo! He's done you again!

AESCHYLUS and EURIPIDES let go of their pans. AESCHYLUS's pan drops lower.

EURIPIDES: Done me? How?

DIONYSUS: He threw in two chariots and two corpses. A gang of Egyptian navvies wouldn't be able to lift that!

AESCHYLUS: Instead of doing this line by line, let him jump in the pan himself. Let his wife and children join him. And all his books. I could still beat him with just two words.

The human scales remove themselves. PLUTO steps forward.

PLUTO: Well? Have you made up your mind?

DIONYSUS: Oh, this is so hard. I consider them both my friends and cannot choose between them. One of them is cleverer, of course, but I enjoy the other one more.

PLUTO: Then you won't achieve what you came down for.

DIONYSUS: And if I do decide?

PLUTO: Then you will return with the winner. Your journey will not have been a waste of time.

DIONYSUS: Thank you, your highness. Well, the reason I came down for a poet is because the city is in a terrible state, and I wanted someone who can give good advice. I think we need to have an extra round.

CHORUS:

Oh Iacchus! Oh Iacchus! Oh!
Oh Iacchus! Oh Iacchus! Oh!

Well, that's a turn up for the books...

The chorus look at each other nervously.

CHORUS LEADER: Um. Sorry about that, ladies and gentlemen. We, er, we weren't expecting this so haven't got anything prepared and it is hard to make up rhymes on the spot, even ones as bad as you have heard tonight. So, anyway, um, round five, um, advice, I guess.

Round Five

DIONYSUS: My first question is about a political leader. One who was elected with a huge majority by claiming the votes of many people who had always voted for the other side. Whilst not currently the leader of his party, there are many who clamour for his return. He's a bad boy without doubt, yet somehow remains popular. Tell us, both of you, what you think of him?

EURIPIDES: I think he has done the city a lot of harm, whilst doing himself a lot of good.

DIONYSUS: That's a fair response. What about you, Aeschylus?

AESCHYLUS: I say that you cannot train a lion cub by letting him run amok and expect him to be tame when he is grown.

DIONYSUS: By Zeus, I still can't decide. One of them speak clearly, the other speaks cleverly. One last question. How would you keep our city safe?

EURIPIDES: I can answer that.

DIONYSUS: Go on them

EURIPIDES: When we trust what we now mistrust and mistrust what we now trust...

DIONYSUS: Just a second. (*Exasperated.*) What? Now you are as bad as him! Explain it clearly.

EURIPIDES: Put it this way. The city will be safe when we start trusting the politicians that we didn't used to trust and stop trusting the politicians that we trust now.

DIONYSUS: That would save us?

EURIPIDES: Think about it. If we are in a bad way because of current lot, couldn't our salvation be by letting the other lot have a go?

DIONYSUS: I see. (*To AESCHYLUS.*) What do you say?

AESCHYLUS: Tell me this. Who do our politicians take advice from? Men of honour?

DIONYSUS: You're having a laugh, aren't you?

AESCHYLUS: Who then? Do they love the slimy and corrupt?

DIONYSUS: They don't love them, but often don't have much choice.

AESCHYLUS: Then who can save a city like that?

DIONYSUS: That's what I'm trying to find out! If you know the answer, you'd better tell me.

AESCHYLUS: If I was there, I would tell you. Down here, I'd rather not.

DIONYSUS: Oh, come on, tell me now.

AESCHYLUS: They will only be saved when they realise that what belongs to their enemy also belongs to them, and what belongs to them, also belongs to their enemy.

DIONYSUS: True, but it is the courts that put a stop to all that sort of thing.

PLUTO: The time has come. You must decide.

DIONYSUS: Very well. It comes down to this. I will let my heart decide.

EURIPIDES: Remember that you swore that you would take me.

DIONYSUS: It was my tongue that swore, not my heart. I will take Aeschylus.

EURIPIDES: What?

DIONYSUS: One of your own lines, I think.

EURIPIDES: You little shit! What have you done?

DIONYSUS: Done? I've chosen Aeschylus; why not?

AESCHYLUS encourages the audience to cheer.

EURIPIDES: And do you dare look in my face? It's outrageous!

DIONYSUS: Outrageous? The audience don't think so.

EURIPIDES: You bastard. You would stand there and leave me for dead?

DIONYSUS: Didn't you once say that life is death and death is life?

EURIPIDES lunges for DIONYSUS and is held back by members of the CHORUS. PLUTO takes DIONYSUS to one side.

PLUTO: Come Dionysus.

DIONYSUS: What is it?

PLUTO: Let us celebrate before you go back.

AESCHYLUS: Let us both go back *and* return.

EURIPIDES: Shut it, arsehole.

DIONYSUS: Great idea.

CHORUS:

Oh Iacchus! Oh Iacchus! Oh!
Oh Iacchus! Oh Iacchus! Oh!

You've made your choice, the better man,
The one who knows what's what,
He'll soon be back amongst his friends,
Leaving the other down here to rot.

You've left behind the poorer man,
The one who's lines fell flat,
He like to think he is so clever,
But he's just a pompous twat.

PLUTO: Well then, Aeschylus. You are the victor. Go happily on your way and save the city with your good advice. Seek out the politicians, the bankers and the marketeers and tell them to make haste. I have plenty of room for them down here.

AESCHYLUS: Thank you, I will. In return, give my place at the table to Sophocles. Tell him to keep it safe, I may be back one day and don't want to see it occupied by anyone else!

PLUTO: You have my word. Frogs! Take it away!

FROGS:

Bre-ke-ke-ke-kex, co-ax, co-ax,
Bre-ke-ke-ke-kex, co-ax,
Bre-ke-ke-ke-kex, co-ax, co-ax,
Bre-ke-ke-ke-kex, co-ax,
Bre-ke-ke-kex, co-ax, co-ax,
Bre-ke-ke-ke-kex co-ax,

ALL

Bre-ke-ke-ke-kex, co-ax, co-ax,
Bre-ke-ke-ke-kex, co-ax,
Bre-ke-ke-kex, co-ax, co-ax,
Bre-ke-ke-ke-kex co-ax.

Bre-ke-ke-ke-kex, co-ax, co-ax,
Bre-ke-ke-ke-kex, co-ax,
Bre-ke-ke-ke-kex, co-ax, co-ax,
Bre-ke-ke-ke-kex, co-ax,
Bre-ke-ke-kex, co-ax, co-ax,
Bre-ke-ke-ke-kex co-ax,

Bre-ke-ke-ke-kex, co-ax, co-ax,
Bre-ke-ke-ke-kex, co-ax,
Bre-ke-ke-kex, co-ax, co-ax,
Bre-ke-ke-ke-kex co-ax.

End

www.ingramcontent.com/pod-product-compliance
Ingram Content Group UK Ltd.
Pitfield, Milton Keynes, MK11 3LW, UK
UKHW020136250726
13967UKWH00002B/685